THE BOOK OF
1 PETER

An Invitation to Form:
Beauty Beneath Sacred Sufferings

Hope Radebaugh

Prayerful Reflections by Dee Kijanko

Contributing Author: Dr. Channon Washington

A NATIONS OF COACHES DEVOTIONAL

The Book of 1 Peter

An Invitation to Form: Beauty Beneath Sacred Sufferings

Copyright © 2024 Nations of Coaches

ISBN: 9798338700273
Independently published.

Front cover image and devotional layout design by Rachel Aponte.
Edited and reviewed by Tanya Cramer.

Contents

Author's Note

What a joy it has been to write this study, diving into the first written work of Peter, the Apostle. There's so much here for us to contemplate, ladies. Because God's truth is eternal, the trials and difficulties those early dispersed Christians were facing (64–69 AD) and the encouragement, hope, and instruction Peter was offering them still impact our lives today in the 21st Century. God's Word through Peter is powerfully and currently alive. The book of 1 Peter is often referred to as the "Job of the New Testament." It is a help manual for our journey in life, particularly those paths on which we experience suffering and grief.

I would suggest the following as a helpful approach to reading this little book: Think of it like a food buffet line. You may be hungry for just the appetizers. Or, you may want the full main course, filling your plate with two to three meats and multiple vegetables. You might even choose to hover around the dessert station, piling your plate high with little morsels of assorted sweets to be enjoyed with an after-dinner coffee. You choose! There is never any shame in coming to God's table. Take as much as you want and stay as long as you'd like. The interesting thing about feasting on God's Word and sitting at His table is this... the more you indulge, the more you want!

God's Word is LIVING. Our triune God in essence is the embodiment of LOVE, LIFE, and LIBERTY! Jesus is our kind banquet master. He sits in the head seat, offering us His heart through His Word. I can almost hear Him saying now, "Welcome in, sit here. I'm so glad you came."

"Look! I stand at the door and knock. If you hear my voice and open the door, I will come in, and we will share a meal together as friends."

Revelation 3:20 (NLT)

Geodes

The pressure is off. The one, true, triune God did some really hard work to reveal Himself to us. His written Word, the gift of His Son Jesus—the giver of Holy Spirit and creation itself—ALL cry out that God is precisely who He says He is. Look around. Evidence of Him is everywhere and in the moment or instance that you don't have your Bible close by for study, you wouldn't have to look far; the things around you, the things He made, all of creation in radiant splendor, displays with heavenly confidence that God can indeed be known and His heart is entirely committed to seeking, saving, and communing with us—humankind—His prize creation.

> *For since the creation of the world, God's invisible qualities – his eternal power, and divine nature – have been clearly seen, being understood from what has been made, so that men are without excuse.*
>
> *Romans 1:20*

So what do geodes, nature's wonder balls, have to tell us about our triune God? What do geodes, these inconspicuous little treasures beneath the ground, have to tell us about Peter's first written work?

Geodes are formed in a couple of ways. They are balls of solidified rocky earth surrounding an inconspicuous inner cavity that can fill with crystals and intricate mineral deposits that form either through the evaporation of water vapor and CO_2 from within, or from mineral deposits that leak in through the outer earthy pores.

Regardless of how geodes form, from crystallization in igneous rock or deposits in sedimentary rock, they are treasures to behold. They are "hidden beauty" beneath the ground. In the words of one (unknown) geologist, "There are plenty of beautiful gemstones out there, but in only one category, the geode, it's what's on the inside that counts. These humble little rocks transform into priceless gems, and it takes a skilled eye to spot these beauties. Geode treasures can even be passed from one generation to the next—little inconspicuous treasure chests with shimmering crystals on the inside. Who knew that just an ordinary rock could contain such dazzling beauty?"

Could your current suffering be leading to the formation of something beautiful deep within? Could your trials and grief be the agents being used by God to shape you— something of priceless worth—that may be passed down to generations to come? Let God form your connections.

GOD ⟶ 1 PETER ⟶ GEODES ⟶ YOU

May God's invisible qualities, His eternal power, and His divine nature do the work deep within, forming you, forming me, forming us—inconspicuous little treasures, deep beneath the ground.

Introduction to the Book of 1 Peter

Perhaps one of the kindest qualities of God demonstrated through Jesus Christ His Son, and empowered by the work of His Spirit, is the perpetual invitation to His people to **FORM**. Evidence is clear. Line by line, verse by verse: Genesis through Revelation reminds us again and again that God is actively on mission with mindful intentionality in the lives of people, nations, and even creation to transform that which is broken into something beautiful. For anyone willing to notice or participate, our joys, sorrows, the mundane, and the extraordinary, all collide on the welcome mat of God's heart with an eternal invite to join Him in the hard work of transformation, trusting and giving Him access to our stories—beginning, middle, and end—come what may.

Form (verb); to bring together parts or combine to create something.

This theme is no different in the book of 1 Peter. Like a beautiful geode forming beneath the ground—a humble rock being transformed into a priceless gem—Peter's life, the life of believers and the early church were all being shaped through the things they suffered. Written around 63 or 64 AD, Peter's first written work can best be understood by grasping the details of the back story.

Let's start with Peter:

- Peter was one of Jesus' 12 disciples. He actually starts this letter by calling himself, Peter, an apostle of Jesus Christ (1 Peter 1:1).

- He was from Bethsaida (John 1:44) and was found by Jesus in the fishing village of Capernaum along with his brother Andrew.

- Peter is mentioned in the gospels more times than any of the other apostles and only second to Jesus himself. Jesus speaks to Peter more often than any of the other disciples and rebukes Peter more often than any of the other disciples.

- Peter's name wasn't always Peter. Matthew 4:18–20 reminds us that he was first known as Simon and that Jesus first called him to come follow, by the Sea of Galilee.

- Peter was married. Matthew 8:14–15 tells us of Jesus going to Peter's house and healing his mother-in-law.

"A humble rock being formed into a priceless gem."

- What a journey! Some of Peter's more "stellar" moments included: chopping off the ear of Malchus the soldier in the garden of Gethsemane (John 18:10), walking on water to Jesus on the sea of Galilee (Matthew 14:22–33), denying Jesus three times before the crucifixion (Luke 22:55–62), naming Jesus as the Son of the Living God when Jesus asked him "who do you say that I am" (Matthew 16:15–16), being told by Jesus that his new name would be Peter (or Cephas, which means "rock") and it would be on that rock that Jesus would ultimately build His church (Matthew 16:17–19).

- Peter had the power given to him by God to heal, even raise the dead (Acts 5 and 9).

- Peter received a vision from God on a rooftop—confronting his pride and prejudices, ultimately leading him to share the gospel message to Gentiles in Cornelius' house (Acts 10).

- Peter witnessed Jesus being transfigured in Matthew 17.

- Peter was called "Satan" by Jesus when Peter tried to deny that Jesus would go to the cross, after Jesus predicted His death in Matthew 16:21–23.

- Historians recount that between 64–68 AD Peter was martyred and crucified upside down, viewing himself not worthy of a "right side up" crucifixion like Jesus.

Context:

Stories only make sense within the context in which they are written. The following is a window of seeing and understanding what the climate was like in and during the writing of 1 Peter:

- Nero was the ruling authority in Rome at the time 1 Peter was written. Nero hated Christians.

- Historians allude to the fact that Nero likely ordered the burning of Rome (which started on July 18, 64 AD and lasted for six straight days) because he had been denied funds by the Roman government to refurbish the city.

- Historians also allude to the fact that to protect himself, Nero blamed Christians for the burning of Rome.

- Fearful for their lives, Christians and those associated with the faith fled to nearby provinces surrounding Rome (modern-day Turkey), in South Asia.

- Between 64–69 AD, during the recording of this epistle, the most brutal and God-forbidden persecution and martyrdom occurred among Christians with recorded historic accounts of Christians even being tarred and burned in Nero's garden as nighttime lanterns. The following is on record from the writings of Tacitus, the historian:

  > Mockery of every sort was added to their deaths. Covered with the skins of beasts, they were torn by dogs and perished, or were nailed to crosses, or were doomed to the flames and burnt, to serve as a nightly illumination, when daylight had expired.

- Thus, enter into the opening lines of 1 Peter 1:

  > Peter, an apostle of Jesus Christ, to God's elect, strangers in the world, scattered throughout Pontos, Galatea, Cappadocia, Asia and Bethynia, who have been chosen, according to the foreknowledge of God, the Father, through the sanctifying work of the Spirit, for obedience to Jesus Christ and the sprinkling of his blood: Grace and peace be yours in abundance.

The words "strangers" and "scattered" make perfect sense against this backdrop

1 Peter is an invitation to FORM through the things we suffer. It is God's invitation to form us and our choice to trust Him through the process—beginning, middle, and end.

11

Welcome in!

I'm so glad you've chosen this journey. May God's timeless, transformative truth shape you much like a geode, prayerfully holding for you the same eternal beauty that it did for Peter and the early church: a humble "rock" gracefully and supernaturally formed; a priceless gem beneath the ground.

EXPLANATION OF P.R.A.Y.

P.R.A.Y. is a tool and format we will use throughout our study which helps us focus on hearing God's voice as we pray, read, and listen.

P - A time of PAUSE, breathing in and out as we calm our bodies, settling into a space of purposeful alone time with God, preparing to hear His voice. This practice is one of STILLNESS.

R- A time to REFLECT on God's Word; more LISTENING oriented as we read and perhaps reread shorter passages of Scripture, trusting Holy Spirit to draw our attention to any words or phrases God could be using to speak to us.

A - A time to seek God through ASKING; more INQUIRY oriented. We ask questions about Jesus, His teachings, ourselves and others, prayerfully listening to Holy Spirit draw our attention to anything we need to say, or anything we need to hear from God. This can include promptings that lead us to confess any known or unknown sin as we continue to grow and learn. We thank Jesus for His forgiveness and help. ASK also includes seeking Jesus' help and intervention through prayerful petitions for others, our families, our world, and ourselves. Think of the ASK section in terms of contemplative questions or thoughts.

Y - A time of YIELDING to the mission of Christ; more ACTION oriented, tuning our hearts and our minds to hear and follow Jesus' instructions. A time of stillness and responsiveness as we YIELD to the promptings of Holy Spirit to ACT. Think of the YIELD section in terms of action steps.

GEODE GYMSTONES

The Geode Gymstones section in this book is specific to the sports life and those who live this lifestyle, offering unique invitations to go deeper in spiritual formation through the shared, common experiences that resonate from being a member of a sports family.

GEODE GEMSTONES

The Geode Gemstones section in this book offers spiritual "nuggets" and invitations to go deeper in spiritual formation through added inquiry for the general audience.

1
1 Peter 1:1–7

PAUSE

Lord Jesus I come before you now, pausing in your presence, asking you to calm my scattered senses. I breathe in and breathe out, recognizing that you are the embodiment of peace. I ask that you open my eyes and my ears and all of my senses, making me aware of your presence and your thoughts in every way. Come, Lord Jesus, come. As I open my heart and my mind to the study of 1 Peter, I need your help to understand. I ask you, Holy Spirit, now and in the coming days, to enlighten my entire being—body, soul, and spirit—to the very specific truths you want me to know. Jesus, would you help me to lean into what you are saying? Jesus, would you help me meditate on the things you are teaching? Jesus, would you help me implement the transformational truths written in your Word so my life would indeed continue to be molded into your likeness? Thank you that you are a truth-telling God and that you have in mind my transformation individually, and the transformation of the world, as I lean in to understand and as I lean out to share with others. Speak to me today through the reading and teaching of your Word. It's in your powerful, precious name I pray. Amen.

REFLECT

In your most comfortable spot with your Bible and pen, ask Holy Spirit to be your teacher as you read today's Scripture passage. Particularly listen for any words or phrases that stand out to you that God may be using to speak to your heart.

1 Peter 1:1–7

[1] Peter, an apostle of Jesus Christ, To God's elect, strangers in the world, scattered throughout Pontus, Galatia, Cappadocia, Asia and Bithynia, [2] who have been chosen according to the foreknowledge of God the Father, through the sanctifying work of the Spirit, for obedience to Jesus Christ and sprinkling by his blood: Grace and

peace be yours in abundance. ³ Praise be to the God and Father of our Lord Jesus Christ! In his great mercy he has given us new birth into a living hope through the resurrection of Jesus Christ from the dead, ⁴ and into an inheritance that can never perish, spoil or fade—kept in heaven for you, ⁵ who through faith are shielded by God's power until the coming of the salvation that is ready to be revealed in the last time. ⁶ In this you greatly rejoice, though now for a little while you may have had to suffer grief in all kinds of trials. ⁷ These have come so that your faith—of greater worth than gold, which perishes even though refined by fire—may be proved genuine and may result in praise, glory and honor when Jesus Christ is revealed.

ASK

1. Christlike beauty often emerges as we learn to TRUST Jesus with our beginning, middle, end—come what may. Think about Peter's beginning back in the introduction (ear chopper, denied knowing Jesus), and now reread verses 1–9. What are some words that come to mind when you ponder what must have happened in Peter's life to transform him in the "middle" of his journey?

2. In this letter, Peter is writing to dispersed Christians, most of which are non-Jewish (aka outside the Abrahamic Covenant). He uses strong words of IDENTITY for these "strangers in the world" (v.1), to remind them of who they are. Name some of the words you notice in verses 1–9 which speak to their unshakable, secure identification as God's chosen.

3. Verses 3–5 are "GEMSTONE-RICH" for every believer—"NEW BIRTH, into a LIVING HOPE through the resurrection of Jesus Christ from the dead…"; "…an INHERITANCE that can never spoil or fade…", "SHIELDED by God's power" just to name a few. What gemstones do you find in verses 3–5? What do these mean to you?

4. In verses 6 and 7, Peter begins to address these scattered, oppressed believers' grief and sufferings with an explanation of why. Frankly, we don't get that very often and we're not promised the understanding of our why's. What does Peter tell them in verse 7 and what is your response?

YIELD

1. Think about your beginning, your middle, and your end. What words come to mind in your current journey of the "middle" you find yourself in? What might God be asking you to yield to Him, TRUSTING Him in the middle?

2. Scripture is clear that God is patient, wanting all to come to repentance, not wanting anyone to perish (2 Peter 3:9). We see in 1 Peter 1:2 that we are chosen according to the foreknowledge of God the Father, through the sanctifying work of the Spirit for obedience to Christ Jesus. God is omniscient (all-knowing), omnipresent (He's everywhere), and omnipotent (all-powerful). He knows all things and delights in our saying "yes" to Him. Check in with yourself and notice the word "chosen." How does that sit with you, that the God of the universe CHOSE you—your beginning, middle, and end—knowing ahead of time that you would say YES! Is there anything about this truth that you wrestle with that you may need to yield?

3. What is God showing you in your current trials and grief regarding trust, specifically trusting Him?

GEODE GYMSTONES

The "brave new world" of college basketball has left us all with a sense of wandering and wondering, feeling "scattered" in a portal world, not knowing from one year to the next—player placement, or even coaching placement. What could God be saying to you today through 1 Peter 1:9 about:

- your true identity?
- your ultimate security?
- how He may be using your grief and your trials?

"It takes a skilled eye to spot these beauties."

—A Geologist

GEODE GEMSTONES

Go back and reread 1 Peter 1:1 and read 2 Peter 3:9, asking Holy Spirit to help you reconcile these two verses. Let God do the work of formation in you as you trust Him.

2
1 Peter 1:8–12

PAUSE

Thank you, Lord Jesus, that you are sovereign. Thank you that you are kind. Thank you that in your greatness, nothing can enter our lives that hasn't been filtered through your hands. Nothing.

I pause before you now, seeking your presence. Thank you that you never leave me and you never forsake me, and that because your Holy Spirit lives within, I can always know that you are near, you are here and present, a friend who sticks closer than a brother. As I calm my scattered senses, leaning into 1 Peter, would you speak to me specifically? Would you quicken my heart to hear your voice and to gain understanding of YOUR LOVE that flows from YOUR very being? Use the pages of Scripture today, your Word Lord, and your Spirit, to transform me from the inside out. Reach deep into the recesses of my heart and align my thinking with yours. I want to know you more, and I trust you to lead me into eternal transformation, looking more like you, learning to love in ways that could only come from you. Have your way in me this day, Jesus. I desire to move forward with YOU, trusting YOU beginning, middle, and end, come what may. Amen.

REFLECT

In your most comfortable spot with your Bible and pen, ask Holy Spirit to be your teacher as you read today's Scripture passage. Particularly listen for any words or phrases that stand out to you that God may be using to speak to your heart.

1 Peter 1:8–12

⁸ Though you have not seen him, you love him; and even though you do not see him now, you believe in him and are filled with an inexpressible and glorious joy, ⁹ for you are receiving the goal of your faith, the salvation of your souls. ¹⁰ Concerning this salvation, the prophets, who spoke of the grace that was to come to you, searched intently and with the greatest care, [11] trying to find out the time and circumstances to which the Spirit of Christ in them was pointing when he predicted the sufferings of Christ and the glories that would follow. [12] It was revealed to them that they were not serving themselves but you, when they spoke of the things that have now been told you by those who have preached the gospel to you by the Holy Spirit sent from heaven. Even angels long to look into these things.

ASK

1. Our Alpha and Omega (beginning to end) God uses all things—our beginning, middle, and end—to form us and His work is ongoing. From session 1, in 1 Peter 1:2, we saw "sanctifying work of the Spirit," and now in session 2, 1 Peter 1:9, "you are receiving the goal of your faith, the salvation of your souls." Would you be willing to share with the group anything you notice in your life as God's SANCTIFYING WORK that is currently FORMING you?

2. The search is over. Prophets of old (verse 10) have long spoken about our beautiful Savior, Jesus. Over 300 prophetic utterances about Him have been fulfilled; see examples in Geode Gemstones. How does it settle in with you that God would (SELFLESSLY, verse 12) use four major prophets and twelve minor prophets in the Old Testament to announce to you and the nations

WHO would come, WHAT He would be like, HOW He would get here, and WHY He would pursue you and a lost world?

3.   In verse 12, an interesting invitation is given to us to become curious about angels (see Geode Gemstones). What do you think Peter meant when he said "even angels long to look into these things" (aka believers' salvation)?

YIELD

1. Reflecting on verse 8, what may God be asking you to yield to in trusting Him with what you cannot see?

2. Understanding more about the prophets and their writings in the Old Testament is a faith-builder in countless ways. Could God be asking you to yield and to dig into the study of the prophecies that were spoken about our Messiah, Jesus?

3. Peter, in verse 12, alludes to the selfless sacrifice of the prophets, describing their tireless and fearless work of proclaiming God's divine and often confrontational messages, without any promise of seeing them come to pass. Because prophets often spoke futuristically, they could die before the prophetic fulfillment happened. Is God pointing out anything in your life today where He's asking you to TRUST Him and continue in your tireless, selfless effort, knowing you may or may not ever see the fruit of that work, at least here on this side of Heaven? How does that settle in with you? Any action steps needed?

GEODE GYMSTONES

The coaching lifestyle is hard and we transition a lot. In our uncertainties, God is so desperately needed to help us navigate this increasingly complex world. Could you name with your group any instance or recall in your life when you believe God may have sent an angel to help you and encourage you?

GEODE GEMSTONES

The first mentioning of Jesus, the coming Messiah, was spoken through Moses by God in Deuteronomy 18:18–19:

> I will raise up for them a prophet like you from among their fellow Israelites, and I will put my words in his mouth. He will tell them everything I command him. I myself will call to account anyone who does not listen to my words that the prophet speaks in my name. (NIV, 2011)

Additionally, Peter our author, in his second New Testament book, 2 Peter 1:20–21, affirms that the Old Testament prophets' divine instructions and inspirations were indeed from God.

> Above all, you must understand that no prophecy of Scripture came about by the prophet's own interpretation of things. For prophecy never had its origin in the human will, but prophets, though human, spoke from God as they were carried along by the Holy Spirit. (NIV, 2011)

The four major (greater in length) prophetic Old Testament books Isaiah, Jeremiah, Ezekiel , and Daniel (additionally, Lamentations, thought to be written by Jeremiah), and the twelve minor prophetic books (shorter in length) Hosea, Joel, Amos, Obadiah, Jonah, Micah, Nahum, Habakkuk, Zephaniah, Haggai, Zechariah, and Malachi ALL speak to us, declaring God's message in ways that encourage, correct, and edify us in our faith.

To stimulate your curiosity, here are just three prophecies (we think over 500 exist in Scripture), that were spoken in the Old Testament that were fulfilled in the New Testament about Jesus and God's kingdom:

1. Prophecy about Jesus' Birthplace

Prophecy: "But you, Bethlehem Ephrathah, though you are small among the clans of Judah, out of you will come for me one who will be ruler over Israel, whose origins are from of old, from ancient times" (Micah 5:2).

Fulfillment: "When he had called together all the people's chief priests and teachers of the law, he asked them where the Messiah was to be born. 'In Bethlehem in Judea,' they replied, 'for this is what the prophet has written: "But you, Bethlehem, in the land of Judah, are by no means least among the rulers of Judah; for out of you will come a ruler who will shepherd my people Israel"'" (Matthew 2:4–6, NIV 2011).

2. Prophecy about Jesus' ministry in setting the captives free

Prophecy: "The Spirit of the Sovereign Lord is on me, because the Lord has anointed me to proclaim good news to the poor. He has sent me to bind up the brokenhearted, to proclaim freedom for the captives and release from darkness for the prisoners" (Isaiah 61:1, NIV 2011).

Fulfillment: "He went to Nazareth, where he had been brought up, and on the Sabbath day he went into the synagogue, as was his custom. He stood up to read, and the scroll of the prophet Isaiah was handed to him. Unrolling it, he found the place where it is written: 'The Spirit of the Lord is on me, because he has anointed me to proclaim good news to the poor.

He has sent me to proclaim freedom for the prisoners and recovery of sight for the blind, to set the oppressed free, to proclaim the year of the Lord's favor.' Then he rolled up the scroll, gave it back to the attendant and sat down. The eyes of everyone in the synagogue were fastened on him. He began by saying to them, 'Today this Scripture is fulfilled in your hearing'" (Luke 4:16–21, NIV 2011).

3. Prophecy about Jesus' resurrection

Prophecy: "I will not die but live, and will proclaim what the Lord has done. The Lord has chastened me severely, but he has not given me over to death" (Psalm 118:17–18).

Fulfillment: "In their fright the women bowed down with their faces to the ground, but the men said to them, 'Why do you look for the living among the dead? He is not here; he has risen! Remember how he told you, while he was still with you in Galilee: "The Son of Man must be delivered into the hands of sinful men, be crucified and on the third day be raised again"'" (Luke 24:5–7).

Time spent studying the prophets and their writings are unmistakably Geode Gemstones!

Now for Angels (created beings who do God's bidding)!!!! Check out these verses for at least four angel types we are told about in Scripture:

- Cherubim: Genesis 3:24, Ezekiel 10
- Seraphim: Isaiah 6:1–7
- Archangels: Jude 1:9, 1 Thessalonians 4:16
- Angels: All throughout Scripture, Psalm 91:11–12 is a favorite!

IDENTITY

Father, You know me!

May I discover the hidden beauty You are forming in me,

Creator of my heart, soul, mind and body,

You created me with true beauty, in true beauty, for True Beauty!

You are the most beautiful of all!

And You created me in Your Image!

May I reflect the beauty of Your Glory, Lord!

May my hardships and sorrows drive me deeper into Your heart of love for me.

I thank You ahead for how You will form knowledge and understanding through the deep faith and words of Peter, the apostle, the Rock.

I trust You to use the things You allow in my life to form my heart to be more and more like the heart of my Lord Jesus.

I invite You to open the eyes of my heart to see how You bring joy out of sorrow,

strength out of weakness,

and glory out of darkness!

You are my HOPE in the midst of my hardships.

You are my example on how to endure faithfully.

You take the joys and sorrows of my life and make good things richer!

You refine and form my character as you make hard things lighter.

You are unfolding beauty in my life.

I praise and worship You my Lord!

In the powerful name of Jesus, I pray. Amen.

A space to journal...

3
1 Peter 1:13–2:3

PAUSE

I pause before you now Lord Jesus, asking you to reveal yourself in the space of my heart, and the space I'm actually in right now, communing with you. Show me and teach me the things you need me to know, helping me calm my scattered senses, and believing in my core that you are who you say that you are, and that I am who you say that I am. Form in me, Holy Spirit, the holiness that you tell me already belongs to me because I belong to you. Help me to understand what it means regarding my purchase—that I was bought, not with cheap things but with eternal things that cost you everything. Would you form these truths in me today, Jesus? I long to understand more about you, myself, and others, that I may live out the holy life, becoming a "spiritual billboard" to those around me, pointing the way to YOU. Trusting YOU, kind Jesus, to do the transformative work in me that only you can do. Amen.

REFLECT

In your most comfortable spot with your Bible and pen, ask Holy Spirit to be your teacher as you read today's Scripture passage. Particularly listen for any words or phrases that stand out to you that God may be using to speak to your heart.

1 Peter 1:13–2:3

13 Therefore, prepare your minds for action; be self-controlled; set your hope fully on the grace to be given you when Jesus Christ is revealed. 14 As obedient children, do not conform to the evil desires you had when you lived in ignorance. 15 But just as he who called you is holy, so be holy in all you do; 16 for it is written: "Be holy, because I am holy."

17 Since you call on a Father who judges each man's work impartially, live your lives as strangers here in reverent fear. 18 For you know that it was not with perishable *things such as silver or gold that you were redeemed from the empty way of life handed down to you from your forefathers, ¹⁹ but with the precious blood of Christ, a lamb without blemish or defect. ²⁰ He was chosen before the creation of the world, but was revealed in these last times for your sake. ²¹ Through him you believe in God, who raised him from the dead and glorified him, and so your faith and hope are in God. ²² Now that you have purified yourselves by obeying the truth so that you have sincere love for your brothers, love one another deeply, from the heart. ²³ For you have been born again, not of perishable seed, but of imperishable, through the living and enduring word of God. ²⁴ For, "All people are like grass, and all their glory is like the flowers of the field; the grass withers and the flowers fall, ²⁵ but the word of the Lord stands forever." And this is the word that was preached to you.*

Chapter 2

¹ Therefore, rid yourselves of all malice and all deceit, hypocrisy, envy, and slander of every kind. ² Like newborn babies, crave pure spiritual milk, so that by it you may grow up in your salvation, ³ now that you have tasted that the Lord is good.

ASK

1. Continue to follow Peter's breadcrumbs: identity, salvation, sanctification, and the witness of prophets and angels regarding Jesus and the salvation of His people. The word "therefore" (v. 13) naturally creates a perfect segway for the mandates Peter is laying out for holy living. Quoting Leviticus 19:2 from the Lord's spoken words to Moses, "Be holy, for I am holy" (v. 16), what specific instructions do you notice (vv.13–16) regarding God's game plan for your life in the formation of holiness? Which one is most challenging for you?

2. Being holy has always seemed like an unreachable mountain summit. Discuss any connections you see in today's reading between setting your hope fully on the GRACE to be given to you when Christ is revealed, and the charge to no longer conform to the evil desires you had when you lived in ignorance (vv. 13–14). What freedom do you find in the fact that, according to Hebrews 10:10,14 (verses referenced in Geode Gemstones), Jesus already declares you holy?

3. Read again verses 17–21. List all attributes you notice in these verses about God and about Jesus. After that, list any gifts you notice coming your way from God and from Jesus.

4. Don't you just love Peter's mandate in verse 22 to these scattered believers: "Love one another deeply, from the heart"? What does loving deeply from the heart mean to you and have you ever experienced or noticed this kind of love? Please share with your group.

5. One of the last challenges Peter issues in today's verses is "grow up in your salvation." What specific behaviors does Peter name saying "get rid of these"? How are we equipped to do this (vv. 2:1–3)?

YIELD

1. As you ponder today's verses surrounding holy formation, is God saying anything to you about yielding in any of these areas?

2. Scripture is clear: as believers we are holy because of Jesus Christ in us, yet we also continue to work out our salvation as Holy Spirit transforms our behavior on the daily. Is there anything God is asking you to take action in today to make a shift in actually believing Hebrews 10:10,14 is true?

3. Are there any heart adjustments that need to be made today that would help you truly believe that the Lord is GOOD?

4. Who in your life might God be saying, "Love that person deeply, from the heart"?

GEODE GYMSTONES

In the [illegible] new world of college athletics ([illegible]), [illegible] instructions to us remain the same regarding the formation of holiness. How could the challenging and changing climate of our industry be shaping your holiness?

For example, What could God be saying to us about loving and pouring into our "ten month" players just as much as "four year" players?

What are some tangibles that would prompt us to enthusiastically serve and love newcomers of any sort (new parents, new coaches, new support staff), regardless of how long they remain on our team?

How are we (I, me, you), managing our anger? It's real ladies!

How can we best establish healthy, good boundaries that are serving to help facilitate emotional safety?

"Be holy, as I am holy." Jesus

GEODE GEMSTONES

Read Hebrews 10 in its entirety. Verses 10 and 14 are particularly important in understanding 1 Peter 1:16.

> [10] *"And by that will, we have been made holy through the sacrifice of the body of Jesus Christ once for all."*
>
> [14] *"because by one sacrifice he has made perfect forever those who are being made holy."*

Discuss how a believer is holy, and at the same time is being made holy.

OR

Read Ephesians 2:1–9.

Compare the writings of the Apostle Paul to today's verses from the Apostle Peter. Record any similarities that you see.

4
1 Peter 2:4–12

PAUSE

Strong Jesus, I thank you that you are the "cornerstone" and the "capstone" of life. Thank you that your strong shoulders are sufficient for holding the weight of every life, the weight of nations, the weight of glory—managing it ALL through the holiness and grace that is found in you. Thank you that your head bore a thorny crown that led to "The Glory Crown," that capstone gem which defeated sin, the enemy, and death itself. Today, as I calm my scattered senses and lean into understanding your Word, would you speak to my heart about this cornerstone/capstone quality held by you and that is also being formed in me and other believers? Help me to see it, Jesus, and to believe you and thank you for the spiritual formation that's transpiring beauty beneath sacred sufferings. We love you King Jesus, our "living Stone," our true cornerstone. Amen.

REFLECT

In your most comfortable spot with your Bible and pen, ask Holy Spirit to be your teacher as you read today's Scripture passage. Particularly listen for any words or phrases that stand out to you that God may be using to speak to your heart.

1 Peter 2:4–12

⁴ As you come to him, the living Stone—rejected by men but chosen by God and precious to him— ⁵ you also, like living stones, are being built into a spiritual house to be a holy priesthood, offering spiritual sacrifices acceptable to God through Jesus Christ. ⁶ For in Scripture it says: "See, I lay a stone in Zion, a chosen and precious cornerstone, and the one who trusts in him will never be put to shame." ⁷ Now to you who believe, this stone is precious. But to those who do not believe, "The stone the builders rejected has become the capstone." ⁸ and, "A stone that causes men to stumble and a rock that makes them fall." They stumble because they disobey the message—which is also what they were destined for. ⁹ But you

*are a chosen people, a royal priesthood, a holy nation, a people belonging to God,
that you may declare the praises of him who called you out of darkness into his
wonderful light. ¹⁰ Once you were not a people, but now you are the people of God;
once you had not received mercy, but now you have received mercy.*

*¹¹ Dear friends, I urge you, as aliens and strangers in the world, to abstain from
sinful desires, which wage war against your soul. ¹² Live such good lives among
the pagans that, though they accuse you of doing wrong, they may see your good
deeds and glorify God on the day he visits us.*

ASK

1. On geodes: "It takes a skilled eye to spot these beauties" (unknown). In
    today's verses, it almost seems like Peter knew about geodes. Verses
    6–8 describe Jesus as "the living Stone" rejected by men, chosen by God
    and precious to Him. Describing us: "You also, like living stones, are being
    built into a spiritual house..." Talk to your group about the spiritual "geode
    formation" that's happening in you.

2. In verses 6–8, Peter, the human "rock," begins to describe Jesus, the "living
    Stone": a stone in Zion; a chosen and precious cornerstone (v. 6); the stone
    builders rejected that has become the capstone (v. 7); a stone that causes

men to stumble (v. 8); a rock that makes men fall (v. 8). Go back in these verses and name the human behavior that causes men to experience Jesus as a cornerstone or a stumbling block. Discuss with your group.

3. Verse 9, to the scattered Christians in Asia minor, Peter calls them a CHOSEN people, a ROYAL priesthood, a HOLY nation, a people BELONGING to God, or God's POSSESSION. How do these adjectives sit with you?

4. After reading verse 12, what are some practical ways you can live such a good life that even pagans, who accuse you, will see your good deeds and glorify God? Would truly believing these words that describe you in question 3 help facilitate this?

YIELD

1. Sometimes when "beauty" is forming in us, it can be hard to notice or even admit that it's happening, particularly with stubborn areas that have existed for so long. Is there an area of beauty that's forming in you that Jesus is asking you to contemplate, yielding to its formation? Thank Him.

2. "Cornerstone" is a structural necessity of great importance in buildings on which everything else depends. Cornerstones support the weight of the entire building. "Capstone" is a stone at the top of a wall or building—or can be used to refer to someone's greatest achievement, or the greatest part of something. Jesus was/is both. As believers, our spiritual house is being formed, the capstone and cornerstone from top to bottom. What encouragement might you give someone today, maybe even someone that's hard for you (maybe in your own family), yielding to Jesus to tell them out loud that you see capstone or cornerstone formation happening in their lives?

3. Is there a conversation that you need to have with Jesus today about anything that's "warring within your soul" that would keep you from doing good among your enemies?

GEODE GYMSTONES

1 Peter 2:11–12 is a "doozy" for those who live the sports life. What kind of behaviors are "warring in your soul," particularity in the environment of sports, that God is asking you to abstain from, so that the pagans may glorify God among you?

GEODE GEMSTONES

Psalm 118:22 is an Old Testament Messianic reference to Jesus becoming the "capstone." Matthew 21:42 is a New Testament reference in which Jesus calls himself the "capstone."

Have fun cross-referencing these verses today in conjunction with 1 Peter 2:7.

Galatians 5:19–25 is a great inventory checklist for the acts of the sinful nature versus the fruit of God's Spirit. Use these verses to compare and discuss Peter's challenge in 1 Peter 2:11–12.

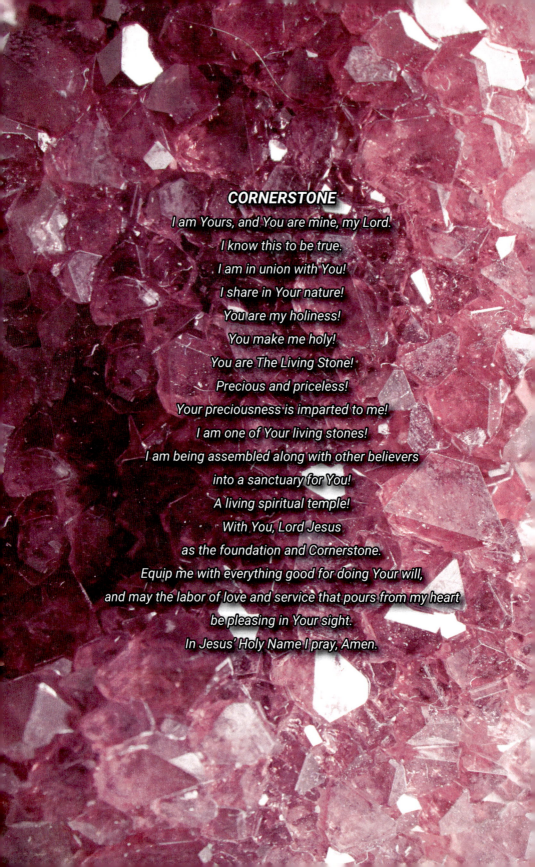

CORNERSTONE

I am Yours, and You are mine, my Lord.

I know this to be true.

I am in union with You!

I share in Your nature!

You are my holiness!

You make me holy!

You are The Living Stone!

Precious and priceless!

Your preciousness is imparted to me!

I am one of Your living stones!

I am being assembled along with other believers

into a sanctuary for You!

A living spiritual temple!

With You, Lord Jesus

as the foundation and Cornerstone.

Equip me with everything good for doing Your will,

and may the labor of love and service that pours from my heart

be pleasing in Your sight.

In Jesus' Holy Name I pray, Amen.

A space to journal...

Session 5 Prelude

1 Peter 2. Slavery and the Bible:
Remember, God is Good
by Dr. Channon N. Washington

As we journey through the Bible, topics surface that will have an emotional impact on us. Some will bring joy and excitement. Other topics may cause fear or even sadness. Today's passage mentions a sensitive topic: Slavery. This may trigger some feelings and thoughts for you. Put your heart in God's hands. Receive His comfort and healing. Let's press into this together.

It is critical that you go into Peter's instructions to slaves knowing that in first century Rome, slavery existed widely and it was brutal. It was not race based. Enslavement came about due to war, trafficking for profit, debt, or in some cases, lineage. It was not always permanent. Even slave rebellions in the Roman empire were not to fully end the institution of slavery but to free only those who were in rebellion. God's Word, through Peter, spoke to the people in the world they created around themselves and in their sinful natures.

For those of us who currently live in the United States, the word "slave" conjures painful images of over 500 years of the specific, brutal enslavement of Africans in the European colonies that would later become the United States. My ancestors, like most African Americans, began their lives in the Western Hemisphere as property, owned by fellow humans.

Slave owners in the United States touted and preached the story of Ham in Genesis 9 and God's instructions to Moses and the children of Israel in Exodus 21 and Peter's instructions to slaves in 1 Peter 2:18. They consistently used these and other Biblical passages on slavery as evidence that God condoned and even encouraged slavery. In what became known as the "Slave Bible," publishers omitted the story of the Israelites' exodus from Egypt or any Scripture that might promote the equality of all mankind in God's eyes. Pro-slavery Americans used that Bible to oppress, obtain wealth, and create a social hierarchy with African Americans indiscriminately at the bottom.

Quakers would be the first Christians to denounce the concept of slavery as a sin against God. As bits and pieces of the Bible were used to justify slavery, the whole Bible would be used to destroy it. It would be Quakers who begin to teach the incongruence of slavery with the equality of humankind in God's eyes. Quakers allowed Holy Spirit to open their eyes to a bigger picture of God's will for His people– all of them. They forbid slave ownership, lobbied the government for abolition, and founded anti-slavery societies based on God's Word and revelation from Him.

To summarize, for the Quakers, the institution of slavery simply did not match the gospel preached by Jesus who said He was sent to free the captives and set at liberty them that were bruised (Luke 4:18). As African Americans like Nat Turner, Harriet Tubman, and Frederick Douglass got ahold of the whole Bible and answered their calling, we start to see both White and African American abolitionists make the case that slavery was a sin against a just and loving God and in conflict with the teachings and life of Jesus.

As a Christian and an African American woman, I refuse to allow the enemy to use any Scripture against me or my emotions. He's been doing that since Eve (Genesis 3:1). He has no creative power so he tries the same tricks with us. Sin was the cause of slavery in the United States. Sins like laziness, greed, and pride disguised as God's will were absolutely Satan twisting the Bible to deceive. Satan wanders to and fro seeking whom he may devour (1 Peter 5:8). Do not allow the enemy to use 1 Peter 2:18 against you, your mind, or your emotions. Satan is the father of lies (John 8:44). Put your heart in God's hands as you go into this study and remember God is good. We see it all throughout the Bible but you also see it in your life and it is undeniable.

1 Peter is about persevering in suffering. On a personal note, I am so thankful that my ancestors did not give up. When I think about reading the Bible and studying its history, I also think about how God instructs us to take encouragement and build endurance from what was written in the past and come together in one mind to glorify God (Romans 15:4–7). I like to believe that my ancestors' endurance cultivated hope in them. I know they also had to have had health too because they kept having babies and kept having babies to get me here today! They clearly believed that the future would be better than the past (Job 8:7). That is nothing short of a miracle. Please remember, we serve a good, loving, and just God (Psalm 33:5).

5
1 Peter 2:13–25

PAUSE

Jesus, I pause before you now asking you to calm and recenter my scattered senses upon your very presence. Help me to lean in to you as I breathe in and breathe out reflecting on the fullness of who you are—Father, Son, and Holy Spirit—in the quietness of this space. Teach me what it means to suffer well in this world in a way that pleases you, transforms me, and glorifies your kingdom on Earth. Today as I unpack these challenging verses, would you give me your eyes to see? Would you give me your ears to hear? Would You give me your heart to understand? Would you give me your will to obey? Create in me a clean heart, O God and renew a right spirit in me, that I may walk in your ways, without restraint, honoring you in all I say, and all I do. May my testimony be a witness of your grace, your love, your mercy, and your power as I learn to trust you more. Amen.

REFLECT

In your most comfortable spot with your Bible and pen, ask Holy Spirit to be your teacher as you read today's Scripture passage. Particularly listen for any words or phrases that stand out to you that God may be using to speak to your heart.

1 Peter 2:13–25

[13] Submit yourselves for the Lord's sake to every authority instituted among men: whether to the king, as the supreme authority, [14] or to governors, who are sent by him to punish those who do wrong and to commend those who do right. [15] For it is God's will that by doing good you should silence the ignorant talk of foolish men. [16] Live as free men, but do not use your freedom as a cover-up for evil; live as servants of God. [17] Show proper respect to everyone: love the brotherhood of believers, fear God, honor the king. [18] Slaves, submit yourselves to your masters with all respect, not only to those who are good and considerate, but also to those

who are harsh. *[19] For it is commendable if a man bears up under the pain of unjust suffering because he is conscious of God. [20] But how is it to your credit if you receive a beating for doing wrong and endure it? But if you suffer for doing good and you endure it, this is commendable before God.*

[21] To this you were called, because Christ suffered for you, leaving you an example, that you should follow in his steps. [22] "He committed no sin, and no deceit was found in his mouth." [23] When they hurled their insults at him, he did not retaliate; when he suffered, he made no threats. Instead, he entrusted himself to him who judges justly. [24] He himself bore our sins in his body on the tree, so that we might die to sins and live for righteousness; by his wounds you have been healed. [25] For you were like sheep going astray, but now you have returned to the Shepherd and Overseer of your souls.

ASK

1. God opposes pride—particularly pride that leads to the oppression of others. It's clear throughout Scripture. However, because of "The Fall of Man" (Genesis 3), His justice and way of bringing forth that justice is often different than it would have been in a perfect garden. Actually, in that garden, it wasn't even needed. In verses 13–17, Peter gives us at least one "why" of God's mandate to submit to every authority instituted among men, "Post-Fall." Reread verses 13–17. Uncover God's "why" and list it here. Why does God ask us to submit to authority, even harsh authority, we may not agree with?

> *"Post Fall" is a reference to the time following the fall of man in the Garden of Eden. It refers to the spiritual climate of brokenness and sin that entered the world once Adam and Eve sinned against God in Eden.*
>
> *1 Cor 14:40; Prov 21:1*

2. God is good. Sin broke this world. Why would God ask Roman slaves to be obedient? Why does God ask us to trust Him and be obedient in difficult times, with difficult people—even with people who persecute us?

3. Verses 23–24 gives us specifics about Jesus, our suffering Savior. Look at each verse and fill in the blanks.

   Verse 23: When insulted, Jesus _____.

   Verse 23: When He suffered, Jesus _____.

   Verse 24: Jesus bore our sins in His body on a tree so that,

   _____.

   Verse 24: Jesus was wounded so that, _____.

   What did Jesus have to know about His father, God, to go the distance in this type of suffering?

4. What exhortation in verse 25 do you find most encouraging?

YIELD

1. Again, today's verses present challenges for almost anyone who reads them. Submitting to harsh ruler/authority for the Lord's sake is "Big Girl" stuff. How might God be asking you to yield?

2. Is there any area of your heart that might require some shifting to be able to trust God to this level?

GEODE GYMSTONES

How do the mandates in 1 Peter 2:13–21 (submitting to all authority for the Lord's sake) filter through your sports life grid? Be mindful that some sports families work in an environment that is a "family-friendly" model and some sports families work in an environment that is a tyrannical "bow the knee to the ball" model. What do you do with this 1 Peter 2 passage as you think about these two different scenarios? Is this even possible and if so, how?

GEODE GEMSTONES

Psalm 89:14–16 says the following:

> Righteousness and justice are the foundation of your throne; love and faithfulness go before you. Blessed are those who have learned to acclaim you, who walk in the light of your presence, O Lord. They rejoice in your name all day long; they exult in your righteousness.

Discuss righteousness and justice as the foundation of God's throne. Reread 1 Peter 2:13–21. Discuss anything you are noticing.

Go on a treasure hunt in your Bible. Find verses that promise how God meets the needs of the "oppressed."

6
1 Peter 3:1–7

PAUSE

Jesus, I pause before you now, thanking you for your steadfast, holy, and loving character. Breathing in and breathing out I ask you to calm and recenter my scattered senses, making me aware of your peaceful, loving presence. I look to you today, Holy Spirit, to be my teacher. Open my heart and mind to all that you're saying, and in today's challenging teaching show me your heart—what you mean by submission and respect. Give me your heart to understand and create in me a willingness to hear you and to listen to you. Thank you that you are a good God. Thank you that you are a God I can trust. Thank you that when I don't understand, you make a way for me in the wilderness. I love you, Jesus, and I long to know you more. In your precious name I pray. Amen.

REFLECT

In your most comfortable spot with your Bible and pen, ask Holy Spirit to be your teacher as you read today's Scripture passage. Particularly listen for any words or phrases that stand out to you that God may be using to speak to your heart.

1 Peter 3:1–7

¹Wives, in the same way be submissive to your husbands so that, if any of them do not believe the word, they may be won over without words by the behavior of their wives, ² when they see the purity and reverence of your lives. ³ Your beauty should not come from outward adornment, such as braided hair and the wearing of gold jewelry and fine clothes. ⁴ Instead, it should be that of your inner self, the unfading beauty of a gentle and quiet spirit, which is of great worth in God's sight. ⁵ For this is the way the holy women of the past who put their hope in God used to make themselves beautiful. They were submissive to their own husbands, ⁶ like Sarah, who obeyed Abraham and called him her master. You are her daughters if you do what is right and do not give way to fear. [7] *Husbands, in the same way be considerate as you live with your wives, and treat them with respect as the weaker partner and as heirs with you of the gracious gift of life, so that nothing will hinder your prayers.*

ASK

1. Today's verses again challenge us with words that can be triggering and difficult. "Submission" comes from the Greek word "hupotasso" which means *to subordinate: to be under the authority of.* This is hard teaching, particularly when things at home are misaligned regarding love and trust. Read Genesis 3:16, God's instructions to Eve in the Garden of Eden "Post-Fall" and make any connections Holy Spirit may be showing you. Could our loving God in His infinite wisdom know something about justice and harmony in a broken world that maybe we don't fully grasp in our finite thinking?

2. In 1 Samuel 16:7, at the anointing of King David, the Lord speaks to Samuel the prophet with these words: "The Lord does not look at the things man looks at. Man looks at the outward appearance, but the Lord looks at the heart." Now, reread 1 Peter 3:3–4. What is God saying to you about true beauty?

3. It is interesting in today's reading that Peter pens six verses to women and only one verse to men. However, six verses of instruction seems quite acceptable when you consider the concluding remarks in verse 7, that our husbands' prayers can actually be hindered when there is a lack of respect in the home! After man's fall in Genesis 3, our good and loving God gives us a roadmap in 1 Peter on how to create meaningful harmony in our marriages and homes. What about submission and respect challenges you?

YIELD

1. Ponder 1 Peter 3:2. Is there anything Holy Spirit is saying to you about how powerful behavior can become while not using words?

2. God wants you to know that YOU are beautiful. You ARE! You're HIS image bearer. Is there anything standing in your way that is a hindrance in you believing this? What steps are you willing to take to make a shift in truly believing God when He calls you beautiful?

3. How could you implement a new prayer strategy that encourages submission and respect on your homefront? What is God saying to you about this?

GEODE GYMSTONES

What makes you a beautiful coach's wife? Find a Bible verse to support that.

GEODE GEMSTONES

Read the Creation and Fall of Man account in Genesis 1–3. Discuss how what God said back then is still impacting us today in our human relationships—particularly in marriage.

TRUST

Father God!
Our Lord Jesus faithfully entrusted Himself into Your Hands,
carrying my sins in his body on the cross,
so that my sin wouldn't count against me.
His grieving heart gave way to a supernatural display!
Instant healing flowed from His wounding for me!
He never sinned.
He never spoke deceitfully.
When verbally abused, He didn't return with insults.
When He suffered through injustice, He did not retaliate.
He faithfully entrusted Himself into Your Hands for me,
for all mankind!
He suffered in my place to leave me an example to follow.
Oh may I be strengthened in power to live honorably and right
in deep gratefulness and obedience for His sacrifice for me.
May the watching world observe kind conduct, actions and behavior.
May my life be full of good choices that reflect purity and godliness.
May my spirit be gentle and peaceful,
for that is where lasting beauty comes from.
For that is Who my Lord Jesus is.
And that is what is precious in Your sight!
For Your honor and glory I pray. Amen.

A space to journal...

7
1 Peter 3:8–22

PAUSE

Jesus, I come before you now thanking you that your Word teaches me how to live. As I breathe in and breathe out, calming my scattered senses, I ask you to recenter me on your presence and help me to listen to you and to obey. Help me to hear your words Jesus, words from the Holy Trinity, words from you, the Father and Holy Spirit. May every utterance that you say to me today through your Word or anywhere else land on a moldable heart. Take my heart Lord and make it like yours. Teach me your ways and give me the desires to walk in them. I can trust you Jesus, and I love you. Amen.

REFLECT

In your most comfortable spot with your Bible and pen, ask Holy Spirit to be your teacher as you read today's Scripture passage. Particularly listen for any words or phrases that stand out to you that God may be using to speak to your heart.

1 Peter 3:8–22

⁸ Finally, all of you, live in harmony with one another; be sympathetic, love as brothers, be compassionate and humble. ⁹ Do not repay evil with evil or insult with insult, but with blessing, because to this you were called so that you may inherit a blessing. ¹⁰ For, "Whoever would love life and see good days must keep his tongue from evil and his lips from deceitful speech. ¹¹ He must turn from evil and do good; he must seek peace and pursue it. ¹² For the eyes of the Lord are on the righteous and his ears are attentive to their prayer, but the face of the Lord is against those who do evil."

¹³ Who is going to harm you if you are eager to do good? ¹⁴ But even if you should suffer for what is right, you are blessed. "Do not fear what they fear; do not be frightened."

15 But in your hearts set apart Christ as Lord. Always be prepared to give an answer to everyone who asks you to give the reason for the hope that you have. But do this with gentleness and respect, 16 keeping a clear conscience, so that those who speak maliciously against your good behavior in Christ may be ashamed of their slander. 17 It is better, if it is God's will, to suffer for doing good than for doing evil. 18 For Christ died for sins once for all, the righteous for the unrighteous, to bring you to God. He was put to death in the body but made alive by the Spirit, 19 through whom also he went and preached to the spirits in prison 20 who disobeyed long ago when God waited patiently in the days of Noah while the ark was being built. In it only a few people, eight in all, were saved through water, 21 and this water symbolizes baptism that now saves you also—not the removal of dirt from the body but the pledge of a good conscience toward God. It saves you by the resurrection of Jesus Christ, 22 who has gone into heaven and is at God's right hand—with angels, authorities and powers in submission to him.

ASK

1. In a broken society, Peter is now getting to the "finally" (v. 8), culminating his previous instructions which signal harmony as a goal worth pursuing in human relationships. He gives nine "do these" statements and five "don't do these" statements. From verses 8–11, can you find and list the do's and don'ts? Circle the ones that challenge you most. Star the ones that you're having victory in right now. Thank Jesus.

2. In the beautiful promise of verse 12, "For the eyes of the Lord are on the righteous and his ears are attentive to their prayer, but the face of the Lord is against those who do evil," what wells up in you as you think about the very eyes of Christ and the very ears of Christ being dialed in to you personally? How does this offer you hope?

3. From verse 15, what does it mean to you to "in your hearts set apart Christ as Lord"? How do you think this would allow you to suffer for doing good, not fear what evil ones fear or be frightened (v. 14), or give a reason to others with gentleness and respect about the hope that lives within you (v. 15)?

4. In verses 18–22, there are many gemstone treasures. What gemstone treasures do you find for yourself? What gemstone treasures do you find about Jesus?

YIELD

1. Look back over your list from question 1 (the circles and the stars). What is God saying to you right now?

2. Is there anything creating a barrier for you in Christ being set apart as Lord in your heart? What action steps might Jesus be asking you to take?

3. Some parts of Scripture are hard to understand. Verses 18–20 are great examples of this. Lean in right now and talk to Jesus about this. Is there anything He wants you to understand about passages we may never understand?

GEODE GYMSTONES

In verses 15 and 16, strong consideration should be given to engraving these words on a plaque and placing them in our sports homes:

Always be prepared to give an answer to everyone who asks you to give the reason for the hope that you have. But do this with gentleness and respect, keeping a clear conscience, so that those who speak maliciously against your good behavior in Christ may be ashamed of their slander.

Discuss with your group any examples of this that you have witnessed in your sports life. Give praise to God for it.

GEODE GEMSTONES

2 Corinthians 5:21 beautifully states, "God made him who had no sin to be sin for us, so that in him we might become the righteousness of God." Discuss the impact of this verse on your identity with your group. Find other verses in the Bible that state the same lovely truth. Write them down.

8
1 Peter 4:1–6

PAUSE

Jesus, I pause before you now, greatly anticipating your presence and noticing you are near. Thank you that you are everywhere—always present, always speaking. There's just something so special about pulling away and spending time with you. Thank you. You are near. As I breathe in and breathe out, seeking your calm peace within and without, would you order my thinking to align with yours? Would you establish alignment in me—body, soul, and spirit—with all that you are, all that you say, and all that you do? I long to be more like you, Jesus. I love you. Amen.

REFLECT

In your most comfortable spot with your Bible and pen, ask Holy Spirit to be your teacher as you read today's Scripture passage. Particularly listen for any words or phrases that stand out to you that God may be using to speak to your heart.

1 Peter 4:1–6

¹ Therefore, since Christ suffered in his body, arm yourselves also with the same attitude, because he who has suffered in his body is done with sin. ² As a result, he does not live the rest of his earthly life for evil human desires, but rather for the will of God. ³ For you have spent enough time in the past doing what pagans choose to do—living in debauchery, lust, drunkenness, orgies, carousing and detestable idolatry. ⁴ They think it strange that you do not plunge with them into the same flood of dissipation, and they heap abuse on you. ⁵ But they will have to give account to him who is ready to judge the living and the dead. ⁶ For this is the reason the gospel was preached even to those who are now dead, so that they might be judged according to men in regard to the body, but live according to God in regard to the spirit.

ASK

1. In verses 1–2 Peter points us to a "geode transforming heart moment." When we embrace suffering, transformation happens. Talk about this with your group. Has suffering resulted in transformation in yourself, your family, or your community? How are you being formed?

2. In our former lives before Christ, sin was home. Much like a hog who craves and loves mud, it's where we lived. Home. Now in Christ, "mud" (sin) no longer feels like home. It feels like mud. Yuck! Our former "mud-dwelling" companions who we enjoyed the "mud life" with may think it strange that we don't like mud anymore or may even "heap abuse on you" (v. 4) because of the shift. Look closely at verse 5. What does God say concerning this? How does this offer you hope?

3. Verses 5–6 once again speak profoundly to the omnipotence (power) of Christ, our faithful judge. What do you see in these verses that encourages you or perplexes you concerning Jesus, our righteous judge?

YIELD

1. What stands out to you in today's study as a "yielding" invitation from Christ?

2. Name any action steps necessary for change to happen as you listen to Holy Spirit.

GEODE GYMSTONES

The sports life can be an arduous and complex journey. Sometimes it's a sprint; sometimes it's a marathon. Either way, contemplate from today's passage your personal sports life journey and your family's journey, noting how God called you out of darkness ("the mud") and has transferred you into His marvelous light. Thank Him.

> But you are not like that, for you are a chosen people. You are royal priests, a holy nation, God's very own possession. As a result, you can show others the goodness of God, for he called you out of the darkness into his wonderful light.
>
> 1 Peter 2:9 (NLT)

GEODE GEMSTONES

Galatians 5:19–23 is an elite spiritual "geode gemstone" passage. Read this passage and note how you have witnessed or are currently witnessing the "craggy ground" (acts of the sinful nature) being transformed into beautiful "geode crystals" (fruit of the Spirit) in the lives of others or yourself. Be specific.

9
1 Peter 4:7-11

PAUSE

Jesus, I pause before you now, breathing in and breathing out, seeking your peaceful, trustworthy presence. Would you help me to relax, knowing that I am fully accepted, fully loved by you, and that you look forward with great anticipation to time together? Help me to believe that about you—that you actually enjoy our time together. It is true. Today, as I read more about you and your heart, your character Lord, from 1 Peter, would you align my behavior and my thoughts with yours? Would you specifically teach me more about the words I say, the things I do, and the attitudes of my heart as I move forward on the journey with you? Please show me any gifts you have given me that I might embrace them, depending on your grace to use them in places needed for the glory of your name. I trust you today, Jesus, to open my eyes and my ears and all of my senses to see your loving, just, unshakable presence that's literally everywhere my eyes can see. In Jesus' name. Amen.

REFLECT

In your most comfortable spot with your Bible and pen, ask Holy Spirit to be your teacher as you read today's Scripture passage. Particularly listen for any words or phrases that stand out to you that God may be using to speak to your heart.

1 Peter 4:7-11

⁷ The end of all things is near. Therefore be clear minded and self-controlled so that you can pray. ⁸ Above all, love each other deeply, because love covers over a multitude of sins. ⁹ Offer hospitality to one another without grumbling. ¹⁰ Each one should use whatever gift he has received to serve others, faithfully administering God's grace in its various forms. ¹¹ If anyone speaks, he should do it as one speaking the very words of God. If anyone serves, he should do it with the strength God provides, so that in all things God may be praised through Jesus Christ. To him be the glory and the power for ever and ever. Amen.

ASK

1. Each day following the ascension of Christ (Luke 24:50–51), the return of Christ grows ever closer (Matthew 24:30). In view of this, Peter issues some behavioral challenges so that we can stay focused in prayer. He exhorts: a) be clear minded, and b) be self controlled. What presents the greatest challenge for you in maintaining a clear mind and operating in self-control? Could you share this with the group?

2. Pause right now. Reflect on who this letter is being written to: scattered believers who are being killed and persecuted throughout Asia minor. Peter drops a bombshell. To paraphrase, ABOVE ALL, love deeply; it covers a multitude of sins. Unpack this as you pray. Think about your behavioral patterns, both good and bad, paying attention to God's invitation to love deeply. What might He be saying to you?

3. Peter exhorts us to use whatever gifts we've received from God to serve others, faithfully administering His grace in various forms. Would you please

encourage your group today by telling them how God is graciously allowing you to use your gifts to serve others? Ladies, this builds up the body of Christ. Please share.

4. What advice does Peter give us in verse 11 regarding the use of our "tongues" and the use of our "hands and feet" to serve? How does this challenge you?

YIELD

1. Go back to question 2. Spend some time today praying and yielding in any area God shows you. Ask God to speak to you, giving you very specific instructions.

2. Hospitality without grumbling (v. 9). Wowsie! Natural tiredness is a part of the stories we live. Is there anything about this that creates curiosity in you, enough to ask God some questions? Is there an invitation to be hospitable that awaits you? Reread verse 11.

GEODE GYMSTONES

As coaches' wives, we are often asked by the Lord and our sports life community to open our homes to others. Discuss among yourselves what this is like for you. Do you like being hospitable? Is it a challenge for you or something you look forward to? Are you challenged by Peter's exhortation to do this without grumbling?

GEODE GEMSTONES

1 Corinthians 12 is a great chapter to study and understand more about spiritual gifts. Every believer is promised at least one! Read 1 Corinthians 12 and discuss with your group the spiritual gifts or any gift you believe God may have given you.

10
1 Peter 4:12–19

PAUSE

Use the space below to write out your prayer to God.

REFLECT

In your most comfortable spot with your Bible and pen, ask Holy Spirit to be your teacher as you read today's Scripture passage. Particularly listen for any words or phrases that stand out to you that God may be using to speak to your heart.

1 Peter 4:12–19

[12] *Dear friends, do not be surprised at the painful trial you are suffering, as though something strange were happening to you.* [13] *But rejoice that you participate in the sufferings of Christ, so that you may be overjoyed when his glory is revealed.* [14] *If you are insulted because of the name of Christ, you are blessed, for the Spirit of glory and of God rests on you.* [15] *If you suffer, it should not be as a murderer or thief or any other kind of criminal, or even as a meddler.* [16] *However, if you suffer as a Christian, do not be ashamed, but praise God that you bear that name.* [17] *For it is time for judgment to begin with the family of God; and if it begins with us, what will*

the outcome be for those who do not obey the gospel of God? [18] And, "If it is hard for the righteous to be saved, what will become of the ungodly and the sinner?" [19] So then, those who suffer according to God's will should commit themselves to their faithful Creator and continue to do good._

ASK

1. "Painful" trial in verse 12 is written in other translations as "fiery" trial. The Greek word for "fiery" is "purosis" which means *ignition, smelting; burning; refined*. It's the literal picture of the smelting process metals go through, heated again and again with ever-increasing temperatures to melt away the "dross" to gain something pure. The blacksmith will do this over and over, until he can see his own reflection in the final product. (Kind of like a geode forming: impurities evaporate, beautiful crystals appear!) What are you going through right now—what is your fiery trial where God is at work in you to create His own reflection?

2. We are told in this passage that if we suffer for the sake of Christ, we are "blessed" and that we are not to be ashamed, but to praise God because we bear the name of Christ. Would you be willing to share with your group something you have suffered recently, maybe because you bear the name of Christ, that you could give glory to God for right now? We join you in thanking Him!

3. In verse 18, Peter is referencing a parable Jesus taught in Luke 13 on the path being wide and the gate being narrow for believers. What encourages you or alarms you about this teaching? Is Jesus being "exclusive" here or wildly "inclusive" by the truth He is telling us? Please discuss.

4. What does verse 19 mean to you? How do you see yourself committing to your faithful Creator through suffering, continuing to do good?

YIELD

1. In your fiery trial, what is Jesus saying to you today about yielding in that trial?

2. Is there anyone in your life Holy Spirit is showing you today that you may want to lovingly encounter, speaking about the path that leads to God through Jesus?

GEODE GYMSTONES

In our current portal/NIL college basketball culture, we now have less time with those we encounter and love. The "brave new world" of college athletics provides for us a whole new opportunity. Discuss any invitations from Jesus you may be noticing, particularly in view of His teaching on the wide and narrow gate (Luke 13).

GEODE GEMSTONES

> Therefore Jesus said again, "I tell you the truth, I am the gate for the sheep. All who ever came before me were thieves and robbers, but the sheep did not listen to them. I am the gate; whoever enters through me will be saved. He will come in and go out, and find pasture. The thief comes only to steal and kill and destroy; I have come that they may have life, and have it to the full. John 10:7–10

Discuss this beautiful passage with your group. What is sobering, yet reassuring, about these verses? What, if anything, alarms you?

FORM

Lord,

I truly do desire to live in harmony with others,

demonstrating affectionate, caring love and kindness.

May I respond with generousity, sympathy and compassion

when someone is in need.

May humility describe my posture

when I love and serve my family and my neighbor.

May I run to You for strength and grace

when someone treats me wrong or hurts me.

May I rise above sin and evil!

I know your desire is for me to speak blessing,

to pray for them over insults or retaliation!

Strengthen me in power in my inmost being, Lord,

to humble myself under Your Merciful Hand,

to ask for Your help to love and forgive as You love and forgive me!

May I always be willing to encourage others

and celebrate with them achievements and successes.

May I turn from what is wrong and cultivate what is good.

May I pursue peace in every relationship and work hard to maintain it.

May my life be living evidence of Your Truth,

and the difference true faith makes in the real world.

And if anyone asks about my kindness, my love, my hope,

may I be ready with joy and gentleness to share my faith

and why I believe.

For Jesus has made it possible to live a life with harmony!

I will embrace His Goodness! His Character!

And find His Beauty and Blessing in every day!

Amen and Amen!

A space to journal...

11
1 Peter 5:1–5

PAUSE

Jesus, I pause before you now. I praise you for being my Chief Shepherd. I praise you for your ultimate self-sustained ability and character to care for all of your lambs and all of your sheep. Thank you. I am your lamb; as believers, we are your sheep. Breathing in and breathing out, would you calm my heart and scattered senses, helping me focus on your sweet presence? Speak to me today in these final exhortations from Peter, and help me to tune my ears and my heart to your voice—your trustworthy voice, Good Shepherd. I love you. I am listening. I long to be shepherded. I long to shepherd—by and through your grace. In your kind, trustworthy name I pray. Amen.

REFLECT

In your most comfortable spot with your Bible and pen, ask Holy Spirit to be your teacher as you read today's Scripture passage. Particularly listen for any words or phrases that stand out to you that God may be using to speak to your heart.

1 Peter 5:1–5

[1] *To the elders among you, I appeal as a fellow elder, a witness of Christ's sufferings and one who will also share in the glory to be revealed:* [2] *Be shepherds of God's flock that is under your care, serving as overseers—not because you must, but because you are willing, as God wants you to be; not greedy for money, but eager to serve;* [3] *not lording it over those entrusted to you, but being examples to the flock.* [4] *And when the Chief Shepherd appears, you will receive the crown of glory that will never fade away.* [5] *Young men, in the same way be submissive to those who are older. All of you, clothe yourselves with humility toward one another, because, "God opposes the proud but gives grace to the humble."*

ASK

A quick recap.

Peter is now starting to "land the plane." The word suffering has been mentioned in this letter more than any other book in the Bible. Through this lens, Peter has challenged us in HOW to LIVE, in HOW to LOVE, and in HOW to SUFFER. Now, focusing his last remarks on instruction given to "elders" and "young men" in a "believing" audience, let's pause and reflect.

What qualifies Peter?
- He himself is an elder (1 Peter 5:1).
- He denied Jesus three times (Luke 22:54–62).
- He was reinstated by Jesus three times on a Tiberian seashore (John 21:15–17).
- His name was changed; Jesus called him "the rock" on which the church would be built (Matthew 16:16–18).
- Peter watched Jesus suffer (1 Peter 5:1).
- Peter was one of the first to see the empty tomb (John 20:1–9).
- Peter was confident he would share in the glory of Christ to be revealed (1 Peter 5:1).

1. In verse 2, Peter instructs the "elders" (from Greek word "presbuteros" meaning *older; senior*), to be "shepherds" of God's flock—those under their care. Previously, in John 21:15–17, in an intimate conversation while having breakfast with Jesus on the Tiberian seashore, Peter learned from the Chief Shepherd what it means to take care of God's flock. In the conversation, Jesus states, "feed my lambs," "take care of my sheep," and "feed my sheep." What part of God's flock are you currently shepherding? How are you feeding, protecting, and caring for lambs and sheep? Please share with the group.

2. How could using whatever gift you've received (1 Peter 4:10a) and serving in the strength God provides (1 Peter 4:11b) motivate you to willingly and eagerly serve others, being an example to the flock (1 Peter 5:3)? Could God's gift to you + God's strength for you = your willing and eager service to others? Please share your thoughts.

3. As believers, we have a glorious FUTURE to look forward to! This earth is not our home—HEAVEN IS! Read 1 Peter 5:4, along with Revelation 7:17. Please share your takeaways.

    And when the Chief Shepherd appears, you will receive the crown of glory that will never fade away. 1 Peter 5:4

    For the Lamb at the center of the throne will be their Shepherd; he will lead them to springs of living water. And God will wipe away every tear from their eyes. Revelation 7:17.

4. In verse 5 Peter addresses young men, instructing them to be submissive to their elders while encouraging "all," both young and old, to act in humility toward one another. There's a big "why" connected to this charge. BECAUSE, "God opposes the proud but gives grace to the humble." Pride = God's opposition. Humility = God's grace. There is no question to answer today for question 4—just a strong recommendation that each of us will memorize 1 Peter 5:5b. Simply stated... God opposes pride.

YIELD

1. Is there anything God is saying to you today about the connection between pride/opposition and humility/grace?

2. Is there a flock out there God is asking you to "shepherd" or care for? OR, is there a flock you've been long overseeing, that God is now asking you to entrust to Him, as HE appoints another to oversee and shepherd His flock of sheep and lambs? Seek God's grace for the desire needed to yield and obey.

3. Being clothed in humility is a practice and discipline that takes time— sometimes a very long time. Is there an invitation awaiting you in the practice of humility?

GEODE GYMSTONES

In the sports life, we have absolutely been given a flock—God's flock—to shepherd and oversee. Revisit Peter's exhortations in today's reading, specifically being mindful of (sports team/sports staff as "the flock"):

- It is God's flock.
- They are under our care.
- We are to serve not because we must, but because we are willing.
- We are exhorted to be eager to serve.
- We are not to be greedy for money.
- We are not to lord it over those entrusted to us.
- We are to be examples for all.

Discuss this with your group. Discuss this with your kids and family. Discuss this with your coach.

GEODE GEMSTONES

We notice in today's Scripture, 1 Peter 5:4, that "a crown of glory" is available for believers. There are actually four other crowns mentioned in Scripture available to believers:

1. Crown of Glory: 1 Peter 5:4
2. Crown of Life: James 1:12, Revelation 2:10
3. Crown of Righteousness: 2 Timothy 4:8
4. Crown of Victory: 1 Corinthians 9:24–27
5. Crown of Joy: 1 Thessalonians 2:19

Discuss these crowns with your group, landing on Revelation 4:10. What does that verse say about what the living creatures around the throne of God are doing with their crowns?

12
1 Peter 5:6-14

PAUSE

Kind Jesus, I ask you to help me to humble myself under your mighty hand, that you may lift me up in due time. I ask you, Jesus, to help me cast all of my anxieties onto you because you care for me. I ask you, Jesus, to help me be self-controlled and alert, because my enemy prowls around like a roaring lion looking to devour me. Jesus, give me strength to resist him, standing firm in the faith, because I know that my brothers and sisters all around the world are undergoing the same kind of sufferings. Jesus, I thank you that you, the God of all Grace, who has called me into your eternal glory in Christ, after I have suffered a little while, will restore me and make me strong, firm, and steadfast again. To you be the power forever and ever and ever. Amen.

REFLECT

In your most comfortable spot with your Bible and pen, ask Holy Spirit to be your teacher as you read today's Scripture passage. Particularly listen for any words or phrases that stand out to you that God may be using to speak to your heart.

1 Peter 5:6-14

6 Humble yourselves, therefore, under God's mighty hand, that he may lift you up in due time. 7 Cast all your anxiety on him because he cares for you. 8 Be self-controlled and alert. Your enemy the devil prowls around like a roaring lion looking for someone to devour. 9 Resist him, standing firm in the faith, because you know that your brothers throughout the world are undergoing the same kind of sufferings. 10 And the God of all grace, who called you to his eternal glory in Christ, after you have suffered a little while, will himself restore you and make you strong, firm and steadfast. 11 To him be the power for ever and ever. Amen.

12 With the help of Silas, whom I regard as a faithful brother, I have written to you briefly, encouraging you and testifying that this is the true grace of God. Stand fast in it. [13] She who is in Babylon, chosen together with you, sends you her greetings, and so does my son Mark. [14] Greet one another with a kiss of love. Peace to all of you who are in Christ.

ASK

1. We have three enemies in this life: the world, the flesh (our own sinful tendencies), and the devil. In this letter, Peter explains that our sufferings are connected to all three. Expect it. Reread verses 6–8. Read it slowly. Name some specifics Peter mentions, telling us how we have victory over our adversary.

2. A wise counselor/friend once told me, "Resisting the enemy is the easiest thing you'll ever do. The name of Jesus is powerful. It's the critical-self within you'll have a hard time getting to be quiet!" Experience has taught me that this is true! Discuss among yourselves how you begin to discern the difference between a critical self and a real enemy who loves to accuse day and night? What biblical truths quiet both?

3. Find the peaceful promises in verses 10–11. Write them here. Contemplate their power and any specifics of what God says will help you and what He says He'll give you as you bear up under trials.

4. In our final verses, Peter mentions his friends: Silas, a woman in Babylon, and Mark as contributors and encouragers to the work. (Theologians believe the woman could have been Peter's wife, or a sister church in Asia Minor. Theologians also suggest that "Babylon" was likely Rome.) He states "…this is the true grace of God. Stand fast in it." Do you believe this? Record your thoughts here.

YIELD

1. What "geode treasures" have you noticed God forming in you throughout the study of 1 Peter?

2. Is there one particular "dazzling gem" that stands out about the others? Ask Holy Spirit to show you what that might be.

3. Looking back on question 1 (facing suffering and enemy attack), is there any area like a yellow caution light in which God is asking you to slow down, yield, and pay attention to?

4. Is there any part of your suffering that you've categorized as, "This is only happening to me!"? Yield that to God and reread verse 9. Ask God to fill you with confidence and reassurance as you combat this lie.

GEODE GYMSTONES

Memorize 1 Peter 5:6–11

GEODE GEMSTONES

Memorize 1 Peter 5:6–11.

LEAD

Father,

Work in me all that I need to be earnest, disciplined,

intentional and purposeful in my prayer life.

Oh how I long to not be pulled in so many different directions.

Forgive me for worrying about so many things.

Instead, in humility, may I run to You in prayer!

For You want to hear my concerns and carry my burdens.

May I be continually growing in love for You, Lord—

with every passion of my heart,

with all the energy of my being,

with every thought that is within me.

May I have the grace needed to love my family, my friends, my neighbor,

in the same way I love myself.

Thank You for the gifts and talents You created in me to bring honor to You.

Oh how I desire to honor and glorify You in all the ways

You designed my heart and body to love others and serve You!

May I serve You passionately with all the strength You give me,

so that in everything

You alone will be glorified

through Christ Jesus, my Lord!!

Forever and ever, AMEN.

A space to journal...

Final Thoughts

There are plenty of beautiful gemstones out there, but in only one category, the geode, it's what's on the inside that counts. These humble little rocks transform into priceless gems, and it takes a skilled eye to spot these beauties. Geode treasures can even be passed from one generation to the next—little inconspicuous treasure chests with shimmering crystals on the inside. Who knew that just an ordinary rock could contain such dazzling beauty? (Unknown)

"Greet one another with a kiss of love. Peace to all of you who are in Christ."
1 Peter 5:14

Contributing Author Biography

Dr. Channon N. Washington is a native of Detroit, Michigan. She began her journey with Jesus as a preschooler raised in a Christian family. She spent 20 years as a public school educator teaching mostly Economics and Advanced Placement United States History. Dr. Washington's first major area of research has been in supporting teachers in professional development toward becoming more culturally responsive. During and after her doctoral work, Dr. Washington became the first diversity, equity and inclusion administrator in Saline Area Schools in Michigan. Channon has been married to Coach Saddi Washington for 25 years and they have two children, Sidney and Caleb.

Channon Washington Sources Consulted:

Cox, T. (2007b, January 24). Why did African slaves adopt the Bible?. NPR. https://www.npr.org/2007/01/24/6997059/why-did-african-slaves-adopt-the-bible

ESV Study Bible. (n.d.). TGC course: Introduction to 1 Peter. The Gospel Coalition. https://www.thegospelcoalition.org/course/1-peter-introduction/#overview

Fry, K. (2023, July 1). Slavery and the difficulty of interpreting the Bible. Reformed Journal.

https://reformedjournal.com/slavery-and-the-difficulty-of-interpreting-the-bible/

Ham , P. (2024, May 20). The "curse of ham": How people of faith used a story in Genesis to justify slavery. The Conversation.

https://theconversation.com/the-curse-of-ham-how-people-of-faith-used-a-story-in-ingenesis-to-justify-slavery-225212

King James Bible. (2011). *King James Bible.* Proquest LLC.

Martin, M. (2018, December 9). Slave bible from the 1800s omitted key passages that could incite rebellion. NPR.

https://www.npr.org/2018/12/09/674995075/slave-bible-from-the-1800s-omitted-key-passages-that-could-incite-rebellion

Strehle S. The Priesthood of the Believers: Quakers and the Abolition of Slavery. *Religions*. 2023; 14(11):1338. https://doi.org/10.3390/rel14111338

The Origins of New World Slavery. Digital history. (n.d.).

https://www.digitalhistory.uh.edu/disp_textbook.cfm?smtid=2&psid=3035

Pahl, M. (2017, January 27). The Bible is clear: God endorses slavery. michaelpahl.com. June 19, 2024,

https://michaelpahl.com/2017/01/27/the-bible-is-clear-god-endorses-slavery/

Wikimedia Foundation. (2024, June 14). Nat Turner. Wikipedia. https://en.wikipedia.org/wiki/Nat_Turner

Made in the USA
Monee, IL
10 November 2024

69369580R00062